nuristan

PROVINCIAL HANDBOOK / A Guide to the People and the Province

Map of Nuristan

Legend:
- Dirt Track
- District Border
- River
- Provincial Center
- City

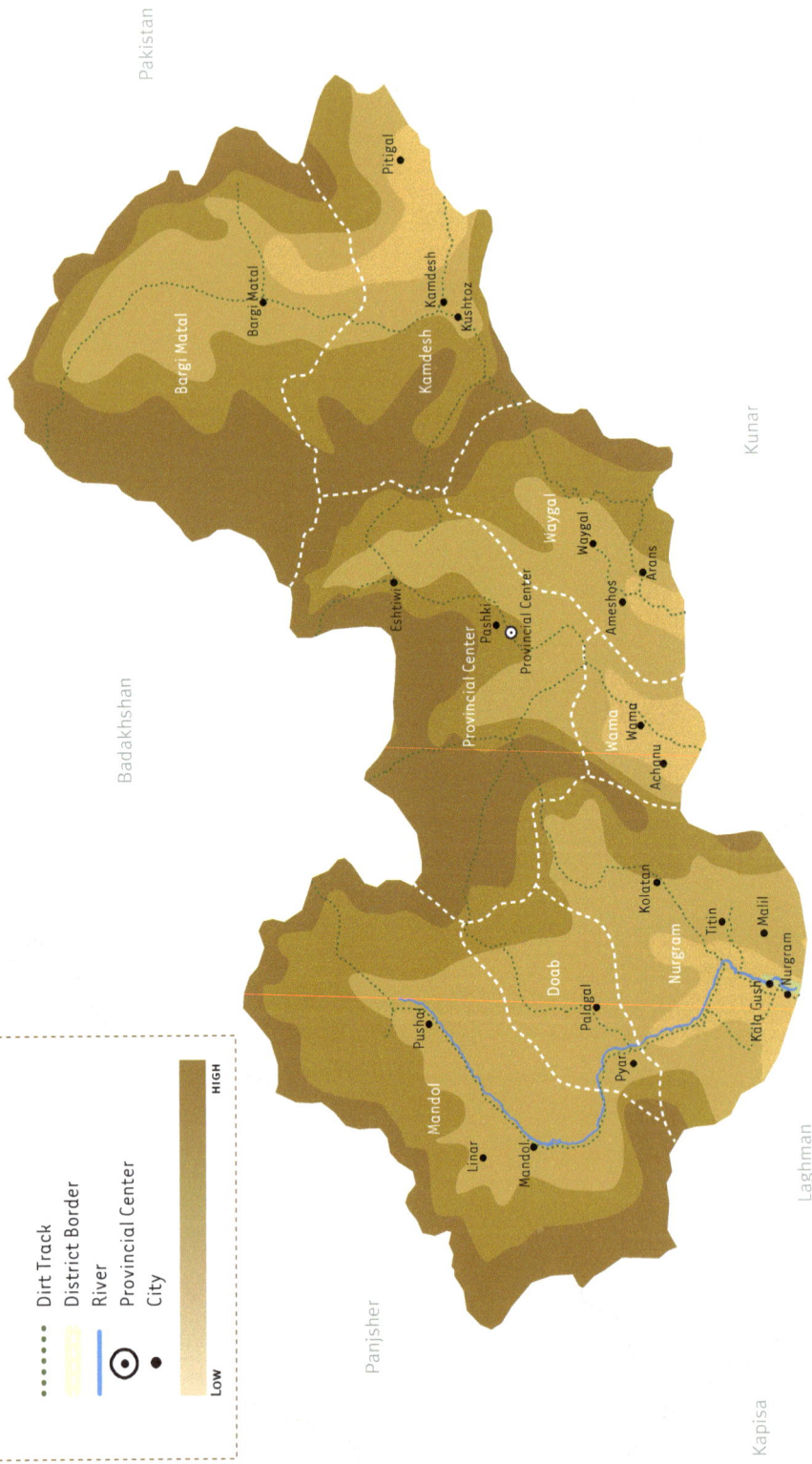

Low — HIGH

Districts and places:
- Pakistan
- Badakhshan
- Kunar
- Panjsher
- Laghman
- Kapisa

- Ptigal
- Bargi Matal
- Kamdesh
- Kushtoz
- Waygal
- Arans
- Ameshos
- Eshtiw
- Pashki
- Provincial Center
- Wama
- Achanu
- Kolatan
- Titin
- Mail
- Doab
- Paigal
- Nurgram
- Nurgram
- Kala Gush
- Pyar
- Pushal
- Mandol
- Linar
- Mandol

Table of Contents

COVER: *Photo by David Katz.*

List of Tables and Maps

LIST OF TABLES

LIST OF MAPS

Acronyms and Key Terms

ABP	Afghan Border Police
ACNP	Afghan Counter Narcotics Police
ADP/E	Alternative Development Program for the Eastern Zone
ADT	Agribusiness Development Team
AICC	Afghanistan International Chamber of Commerce
AISA	Afghanistan Investment Services Association
ANA	Afghan National Army
ANP	Afghan National Police
AWCC	Afghan Wireless Communication Company
BEFA	Basic Education for Afghanistan
BHC	Basic Health Center
CA	Civil Affairs
CDCs	Community Development Councils
CERP	Commander's Emergency Response Program
CHC	Comprehensive Health Center
COIN	Counter Insurgency
CSO	Central Statistics Office
DDS	District Development Shura
DIAG	Disbandment of Illegal Armed Groups
DoS	US Department of State
FATA	Federally Administered Tribal Areas
FOB	Forward Operating Base
GIRoA	Government of the Islamic Republic of Afghanistan
Hezbis	Hezb-e Islami ("Islamic Party")
HIG or HIH	Hezb-e Islami Gulbuddin ("Islamic Party" formed by Gulbuddin Hekmatyar)
HIK	Hezb-e Islami Khalis ("Islamic Party" formed by Mohammad Yunus Khalis)
HP	Health Post
HTS	Human Terrain System
ICRC	International Committee of the Red Cross

IDLG	Independent Directorate for Local Governance
IED	Improvised Explosive Device
IMC	International Medical Corps
IO	International Organization
IRoA	Islamic Republic of Afghanistan
ISAF	International Security Assistance Force
ISI	Inter Service Intelligence (Pakistan)
Jamiatis or JI	Jamiat-e Islami ("Islamic Union")
MADERA	Mission d'Aide au Développement des Economies Rurales en Afghanistan
Meshrano Jirga	Elders' Assembly, upper house of Afghan National Assembly
MRRD	Ministry of Rural Rehabilitation and Development
MoE	Ministry of Education
MoI	Ministry of the Interior
MoPH	Ministry of Public Health
MoPW	Ministry of Public Works
Mustafiat	Department of Finance
NATO	North Atlantic Treaty Organization
NDS	National Directorate for Security
NGO	Non-Governmental Organization
NSP	National Solidarity Program
NWFP	North West Frontier Province
PC	Provincial Council
PDC	Provincial Development Council
PRT	Provincial Reconstruction Team
RAH	Reconstruction Agency of Hindu Kush
SCA	Swedish Committee for Afghanistan
UN	United Nations
UNAMA	United Nations Assistance Mission in Afghanistan
UNOPS	United Nations Office for Project Services
USACE	US Army Corp of Engineers
USAID	US Agency for International Development
USDA	US Department of Agriculture
USG	United States Government
VOA	Voice of America
Wali	Governor
Wolesi Jirga	People's Assembly, lower house of Afghan National Assembly
Woluswal	District Administrator

Guide to the Handbook

This handbook is a concise field guide to Nuristan for internationals deploying to the province. Field personnel have used these guides in Afghanistan since June 2008 to accelerate their orientation process and to serve as a refresher on different aspects of the province during their tour.

Reading this book will provide a basic understanding of the people, places, history, culture, politics, economy, needs, and ideas of Nuristan. Building upon this understanding can help you:

- build rapport and a regular dialogue with local leaders;

- plan and implement pragmatic strategies (security, political, economic) to address sources of instability;

- influence communities to support the political process, not the insurgents; and

- build the capacity and legitimacy of a self-sufficient Afghan government and economy.

As you read the handbook and continue your inquiry in the province, seek to understand the influential leaders and groups in your local area and what beliefs and relationships drive their behavior. Think about the sources of violence in the area and whether groups are pursuing interests in a way that promotes conflict or stability. Finally, consider how various types of activities – key leader engagement, development assistance, security operations, security assistance, or public diplomacy – can effectively influence communities to work within the political process and oppose insurgency.

Sources and Methods

These handbooks are not intended as original academic research but as concise, readable summaries for practitioners in the field. The editorial team relies on their collective field experience and knowledge of the province as well as key sources such as the official Islamic Republic of Afghanistan (IRoA), United Nations, and United States Government (USG) publications, and those sources listed in the appendix.

The editors have made every effort to ensure accuracy. It should be noted, however, that there is often considerable disagreement regarding what is "ground truth" in Nuristan, and things are constantly changing. As such, consider this book part of your orientation and not an all-inclusive source for everything you need to know.

Information in this handbook is unclassified. The views and opinions expressed in this handbook are those of IDS International and in no way reflect the views of the United States Government or the United States Army.

The Electronic Update

Look for electronic updates to this book at *www.idsinternational.net/ afpakbooks*. Updates will cover any new developments, issues, and leaders that have emerged after publication. They will also provide corrections and expanded content in key areas based on feedback from readers.

We hope the handbook will continue to be a valuable tool in thinking about the challenges in Nuristan. If you have questions, comments or feedback for future updates or editions please email afpakbooks@idsinternational.net.

ABOUT IDS INTERNATIONAL

Publisher of Afghanistan Provincial Handbook Series and the FATA/NWFP Pakistan Books

This book is part of a series of handbooks on Afghanistan and Pakistan provinces and regions. Other titles include Ghazni, Helmand, Khandahar, Khost, Kunar, Laghman, Nangarhar, Nuristan, Paktika, and Paktya, as well as NWFP and FATA.

In addition to publishing these handbooks, IDS International provides training and analysis to government and private organizations in the areas of politics, economics, culture, stability operations, reconstruction, counterinsurgency, and interagency relations. In particular, IDS is a leading trainer of the US military in working with Provincial Reconstruction Teams (PRTs) in Iraq and Afghanistan. IDS offers its clients expertise and experience in the difficult work of interagency collaboration in complex operations. The writers and editors on this project offer a lifetime of experience working in these provinces and share a dedication to bringing peace and prosperity to the people of Afghanistan.

Author: Richard F. Strand
Editors: Nick Dowling and Tom Praster
Assistant Editors: Tom Viehe and Chris Hall

IDS INTERNATIONAL GOVERNMENT SERVICES

1916 Wilson Boulevard

Suite 302

Arlington, VA 22201

703-875-2212

www.idsinternational.net

afpakbooks@idsinternational.net

Published: June 2009

This and other AfPak handbooks may be bought in either hard copy, digital, or audiobook format. Samples are available upon request. IDS International is also a leading provider of training and support on the cultural, political, economic, interagency, and information aspects of conflict. Direct all inquires to *afpakbooks@idsinternational.net* or call 703-875-2212.

Nuristan's mountainous terrain impedes the development of roads and communication, making it difficult to extend the Afghan government's presence throughout the province.

PHOTO BY DAVID KATZ

Chapter 1
Overview and Orientation

Nuristan is a land apart from the rest of Afghanistan. The forests, mountain pastures, and steep valleys of the eastern Hindu Kush mountains are home to an ethnically and linguistically unique group of peoples whose Hindu-like ancestors fled and resisted Islam as it spread eastward across ancient Afghanistan. After being driven from Nangarhar around 1000 AD, the Nuristani peoples migrated to the remote upper Pech and Waygal Valleys in Nuristan's central region, from which they expanded into adjacent valleys to the east and west in the higher Hindu Kush range. Their well-adapted subsistence on agriculture and dairying allowed them to remain economically and politically independent in their highland fastness until their defeat by Afghanistan's ruler in 1896.

That defeat entailed the Nuristanis' conversion from their ancient religion to Islam. Although today's Nuristanis have been fully incorporated into the Sunni Muslim community for several generations, their late conversion continues to impart a negative ethnic stereotype to some of Afghanistan's Pashtun (Pashto-speaking, "ethnic" Afghan) and Farsiwan (Farsi/Dari-speaking) citizens. Nuristanis are sometimes subjected to discrimination in areas outside Nuristan, and their homeland has been chronically deprived of development funds. Pashtun and Farsiwan perceptions of Nuristan usually do not accurately reflect the reality of Nuristan, and almost nothing one hears about Nuristan from an Afghan or Farsiwan is true.

For their part, Nuristanis generally maintain a friendly wariness toward outsiders and regard the national government's administration and borders as irrelevant nuisances. Nuristanis view their region as consisting of some 15 distinct Nuristani peoples who each occupy well-defined territories not shown on official maps. They speak five distinct languages and are all hostile to surrounding and encroaching Pashtuns, Gujars, and Panjshiris.

Ethnic prejudices do not, however, preclude individuals of differing ethnicities from forming close friendships or alliances based on mutual respect. A few Nuristanis have risen to the highest levels of national government.

An expanding population, recurrent drought, environmental degradation, monetary exploitation of resources, the persistent influence of foreign-trained jihadist mullahs, and quickening development all impact Nuristani society today. Traditional Nuristani settlement patterns are changing rapidly as populations expand out of compact villages and into smaller dispersed communities that were formerly outlying farmlands. For women in some areas, revenues from exports or remittances have greatly lightened their burden as subsistence-agricultural workers, allowing them to buy food or grow it with wage labor.

Nuristan's mountainous terrain has impeded the development of roads and communication, making it difficult to extend the province's administration effectively into all districts. A continuing jihadist insurgency against the national government has hindered development throughout the province in recent years, leaving Nuristan among Afghanistan's least-developed provinces.

However, the mountainous, difficult land is also blessed with water, trees, and minerals, making it a place where life is harsh but occasionally quite enjoyable.

ORIENTATION

Nuristan lies on the southern slopes of the Hindu Kush mountains in northeastern Afghanistan. It encompasses the watersheds of the upper Alingar (Laghman) River in western Nuristan, the upper Pech River in central Nuristan, and the Landay Sin River in eastern Nuristan. It lies between latitude 34°70' and 38°00' N and longitude 70°00' and 71°40' E. Provinces of Afghanistan that border Nuristan include Badakhshan on the north, Panjshir on the west, Laghman on the southwest, and Kunar on the southeast. Eastern Nuristan borders on the district of Chitral in Pakistan's northernmost North West Frontier Province (NWFP).

The province's southern boundary is incorrectly drawn on Afghanistan Information Management Services (AIMS) and other maps, according to Islamic Republic of Afghanistan (IRoA) sources. These show the Kordar Valley and the lower Waygal Valley as being in Kunar Province's Pech District, and they show the upper Tregam valley in Kunar's Asadabad District. These three areas are technically part of Nuristan province. When working along Nuristan's southern border, ISAF personnel should ask locals which province they are operating in (see Chapter 7 under "Bad Maps" for more discussion of inaccurate maps).

Map 1. Population Map of Nuristan

Legend:
- Dirt Track
- District Border
- River
- Provincial Center
- City

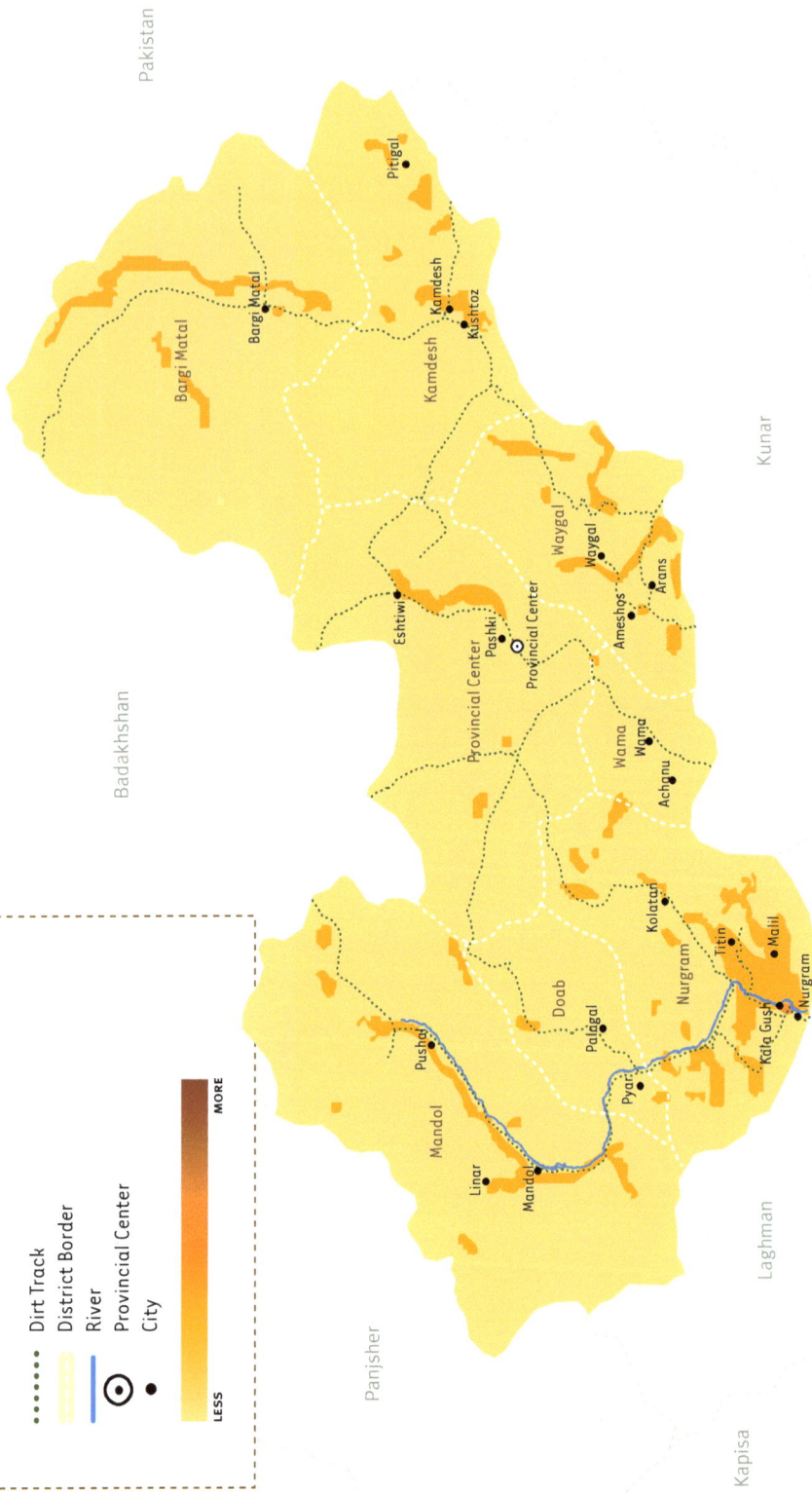

LESS — MORE

Labels on map:

Pakistan

Pitigal

Bargi Matal

Bargi Matal

Kamdesh

Kamdesh

Kushtoz

Kunar

Waygal

Waygal

Eshtiwi

Pashki

Provincial Center

Provincial Center

Ameshos

Arans

Wama

Wama

Achpnu

Badakhshan

Kolatan

Titin

Malil

Nurgram

Nurgram

Doab

Palgal

Kdlə Gush

Pushol

Pyar

Mandol

Linar

Mandol

Panjsher

Laghman

Kapisa

Nuristan's terrain ranges in altitude between 1,000 meters in its lower southern valleys to peaks of over 6,000 meters along the crest of the Hindu Kush mountains, which forms Nuristan's northern border with Badakhshan.

The Nuristanis inhabit the land up to around 4,000 meters in the highest alpine pasturelands. An abundance of alpine grassland above the tree line provides about half the Nuristanis' subsistence, after it is converted to milk by their grazing goats and cows. Those Nuristanis whose lands straddle the lower valleys let their goats feed on the vegetation there during the winter, while the inhabitants of the upper valleys must gather grass throughout the summer to store for stall feeding during their snowbound winters. Agricultural lands are on terraces or relatively flat terrain with good sources of water for irrigation of crops, which constitute the other half of the Nuristanis' subsistence. Villages are often sited on steeper terrain close to the villagers' fields.

Water from spring and summer rains and the winter snowpack sustains Nuristan's primary resource, its trees. Forests of deodar cedar, pine, and fir cover much of the province between the altitudes of 2,100 and 3,200 meters, while evergreen oak and deciduous trees cover the valley slopes below 2,100 meters. In recent decades, much of the slow-growing evergreen-oak cover has been cut down for firewood, and the deodars have fallen to the chainsaws of timber smugglers, leaving the more accessible valleys barren.

Districts

Afghanistan's communist regime of the 1980s declared Nuristan a province, but provincial governance was minimal in the ensuing chaotic years. In 2002 the provincial administration was reactivated and provincial and district boundaries were drawn to coincide with certain traditional ethnic boundaries. The boundaries and number of districts have fluctuated since 2002 and are not permanently settled, reflecting the growing pains of the newly created province. Currently there are seven districts plus one unnamed central region that is administered directly from the provincial center located in the southern Parun Valley near the village of Pashki.

The 2002 provincial boundary leaves some Nuristani lands cut off in Bar Kunar and Naray districts of Kunar province. Nuristanis argue that this boundary will allow Pashtuns and Gujars in Kunar province to seize their traditional lands. Further negotiations will decide whether Naray district remains in Kunar or gets transferred to Nuristan.

District data appears in Table 1.

Key Towns

Nuristanis occupy about 170 communities, which range in size from a few dozen to some five thousand inhabitants. Larger communities often consist of smaller ones, which are designated directionally as the "upper," "lower," "inner," etc., communities. Community boundaries are not always apparent to outsiders, and ISAF personnel should ask locals which community they are actually operating in. No accurate census of the region exists; Afghanistan's Central Statistics Office (CSO) 2005 population estimate is 125,700 total inhabitants for the province. Major communities are listed in Tables 2-4.

Table 1. Districts of Nuristan Province

CURRENT DISTRICT NAME	FORMER DISTRICT NAME	PROVINCIAL REGION	POPULATION (2005 CSO EST.)	CENTER	ETHNIC GROUPS
Provincial Center			11,700	near Pashki	Vasi, Kata
Wama	Wama	Central	9,600	Wama Woluswali	Kata, Sanu, Kalasha, Pashai
Waygal	Waygal		17,000	Want	Kalasha: Vai, Chima-Nishei; Tregami
Kamdesh	Kamdesh	Eastern	21,900	Kamdesh Woluswali	Kom, Mumo, Kata, Kshto, Binio, Jamcho, Jashi
Bargi Matal	Bargi Matal		13,400	Bargi Matal	Kata
Nurgram	Nuristan	Western	28,100	Nurgram	Ashkun, Pashai, Pashtun
Doab			6,800	Doab	Kata, Ashkun, Pashai
Mandol	Mandol		17,200	Mandol	Kata, Pashai
Naray/Ghaziabad (under consideration)	Naray	Eastern	56,173	Naray	Kom, Jashi, Gawar, Mashwani Pashtun, Gujar

Table 2. Key Communities in Nuristan's Central Region

NATIONAL NAME	LOCAL NAME	ETHNIC GROUP	DISTRICT
Gambir	gambir	Tregami	Waygal
Want	vant	Vantä	Waygal
Nishe'i	nisheigram	Kalasha: Nishei	Waygal
Arans	zhonchigal	Kalasha: Vai	Waygal
Ameshos	ameshdesh	Kalasha: Vai	Waygal
Waygal	vaigal	Kalasha: Vai	Waygal
Wama	sama	Sanu (Wamai)	Wama
Achanu	gramsana gram	Gramsana	Wama
Kantiwa Sufla	ktivi	Kata	Provincial Center
Pashki	ushiut	Vasi	Provincial Center
Eshtiwe	shupu	Vasi	Provincial Center

Table 3. Key Communities in Nuristan's Eastern Region

NATIONAL NAME	LOCAL NAME	ETHNIC GROUP	DISTRICT
Pitigal	pitigal	Kom	Kamdesh
Kamu	kamu	Kom	Kamdesh
Kamdesh	kombrom	Kom	Kamdesh
Mandagal Sufla	mumorm	Mumo	Kamdesh
Paprok	peruk	Kata	Kamdesh
Badmuk	badamuk	Kata	Bargi Matal
Barg-i Matal	bragamatol	Kata	Bargi Matal

Table 4. Key Communities in Nuristan's Western Region

NATIONAL NAME	LOCAL NAME	ETHNIC GROUP	DISTRICT
Nangarach	nangaraj	Pashaî	Nurgram
Malil	malil	Pashaî	Nurgram
Titin	titin	Ashkun	Nurgram
Kolatan	kolatan	Ashkun	Nurgram
Palagal	pargal	Kata	Doab
Pyar	pior	Pashaî	Doab
Nilaw	pegal	Kata	Doab
Anish	anish	Kata	Mandol
Kiwisht	kivisht	Kata	Mandol
Mandol	maniul	Kata	Mandol
Linar	linar	Kata	Mandol
Gadwal	gadu	Kata	Mandol
Pushal	pushol	Kata	Mandol

RELEVANT HISTORICAL ISSUES

Provincial/Regional History Pre-1978

Despite persistent legends, Nuristanis are not remnants of Alexander the Great's Greeks or long-lost Arabs. Rather, they are Indo-Iranian-speaking peoples whose languages trace back over 6,000 years from the same Indo-European parent language as have English, Spanish, and some 140 other languages.

For almost 900 years these peoples lived independently in the region, which was called *Kafiristan* ("Land of Infidels") by the surrounding Muslims. In 1895-96 the Afghan ruler Abdur Rahman Khan conquered them and compelled them to convert to Islam. He incorporated the region into Afghanistan and renamed it *Nuristan,* "Land of Light."

Inter-ethnic wars flared up between the Kom and Kushtozi during 1929 and 1998. During the past century the gradual influx of highland Gujar and Mashwani Pashtun peoples into the pasturelands of the Kom and Kalasha spawned sporadic hostilities, which persist to today.

Communist Era (1978-1992)

Afghan communists deposed the government in a military coup in April 1978, and within five months the Nuristanis of the Landay Sin Valley rose up and began the sustained insurgency that eventually drove the communists from eastern Afghanistan. The grassroots anti-communist resistance in eastern Nuristan was splintered and co-opted by the "Seven-Party" mujahedin groups operating out of Pakistan, under control from Pakistan's Inter-Services Intelligence (ISI).

Mujahedin and Taliban (1992-2001)

In 1992 the communist government fell to the mujahedin. In the aftermath, local mujahedin commanders of two main parties, Gulbuddin Hekmatyar's *Hezb-e Islami* ("Islamic Party," also known as HIG or Hezbis) and the *Jamiat-e Islami* ("Islamic Union," also known as JI or Jamiatis), took control in most regions of Nuristan. In Bargi Matal district and parts of Waygal district, Arab-backed Salafi clerics (known pejoratively as *Wahhabis*) had already taken control in the early 1980s.

The Jamiatis became the Northern Alliance and form a major faction of today's national government. Gulbuddin and his Hezbis allied themselves with the Taliban and al-Qaeda and remain the foremost combatants against the national government and ISAF operations in Nuristan today. After coming to power in 1996, the Taliban were unable to extend effective control over Nuristan. Nuristani areas controlled by Jamiati commanders were allied with the Taliban's enemies, the Northern Alliance. The situation favored Hezbi commanders, notably Mullah Sadiq in Kamdesh and Haji Ghafur in Kantiwa, who sometimes acted as proxies for the Taliban while maintaining their independent power through shakedowns and intimidation.

Likewise, the Salafi clerics of Bargi Matal district cooperated with the Taliban, as well as with other Pakistani-run jihadist groups that operated in Kashmir. With the Taliban's blessing, Pakistan's ISI set up training camps in Bargi Matal district for terrorists heading to Kashmir.

In 1998, the villages of Kamdesh and Kushtoz in Nuristan's Kamdesh district fought a war over water rights. The Kamdeshis won by burning the village of Kushtoz to the ground, forcing the Kushtozis to seek refuge in other villages in Kunar and Nuristan. During this period other inter-village hostilities occurred, notably between the villages of Waygal and Arans in Waygal district and Junia and Pyar in Doab district.

Contemporary Events (2002-Present)

After Afghan and ISAF troops forced the Taliban out in the wake of 9/11, the Hezbi commanders and jihadist clerics went underground. The Hezbis and other jihadists (Ishatis, Panj-piris, neo-Taliban, etc.) formed small insurgent cells in various hideouts in the hinterland, harassing local traffic and assistance projects. Cells targeted pro-government leaders and workers with landmines and improvised explosive devices (IEDs). Many non-combatants were harmed or killed.

ISAF troops responded to the Hezbi violence through raids that caused civilian casualties but removed few insurgent leaders. Such raids actually aided the insurgents by engendering pockets of ill-will among a populace generally supportive of ISAF efforts.

Traffic on the Landay Sin road continues to be disrupted by insurgents at numerous makeshift checkpoints along the routes. They use IEDs and RPGs to destroy vehicles, and they occasionally beat or murder transport drivers and road-construction workers in an attempt to cut ISAF supply routes. In parts of the province, insurgents intimidate entire villages.

In addition to local Nuristani Hezbis, external groups of Taliban- and Pakistan-controlled al-Qaeda cells also operate in the region, sometimes in conjunction with the Hezbis. The American presence in Nuristan has become a magnet for jihadists wanting to draw "infidel" blood.

Since 2006 ISAF forces have maintained a presence at numerous outposts in the province, along with their Afghan National Army (ANA) counterparts. Attempts by ISAF personnel to create closer ties with the people of Nuristan looked promising, with the formation of a "100-man shura" in eastern Nuristan in 2007. Diminished follow-through led to a stagnation of the relation-building process by late 2008.

Relations further deteriorated after numerous civilian casualties from ISAF operations in Kamdesh, Doab, and Waygal districts in 2007 and 2008. Responding to casualties in their district in mid-2008, elders from Waygal asked ISAF to cease all operations in the district.

The first half of 2009 saw little positive change in the situation in Nuristan. Outposts in Kamdesh district continued to incur almost daily attacks. In March, while seeking to expand ISAF engagement into the inaccessible western valleys of Nuristan, a convoy from the PRT in Kala Gush came under extended attack after supposedly successful discussions with local officials in Doab district.

Current unrest is an outgrowth of the recent anti-communist war, but contentious groups and factions endure from earlier times. From pre-Islamic times there has been hostility between Nuristanis and neighboring Pashtuns and Panjshiris. Among the Nuristani peoples, the Kata, Kushtozi, and Wamai maintain a longstanding enmity with the Kom.

After the war, one party predominated: *Hezb-e Islami Gulbuddin* (HIG), which, along with other jihadists, controls the persistent insurgency in Nuristan today.

Since the Taliban's fall, Nuristanis and government supporters have been harassed and occasionally murdered by insurgent forces. In addition to relentless hostilities, recurrent drought and increased population have provoked ongoing water wars between the villages of Kamdesh and Kushtoz in Kamdesh district and between the villages of Waygal and Arans in Waygal district.

Nuristanis have become more conservative in their Islamic beliefs. However, the clout of Pakistani and jihadist mullahs has led to a "culture war" between these mullahs and advocates of traditional Nuristani culture.

PHOTO BY DAVID KATZ

Chapter 2
Ethnicity, Tribes,
Languages and Religion

Nuristan is the most linguistically and ethnically diverse province in Afghanistan, comprising some eighteen peoples speaking nine separate languages. The languages and cultures of the Nuristani peoples differ markedly from those of the surrounding Pashtuns and Tajiks. Due to these differences and the Nuristanis' relatively late acceptance of Islam, Afghanistan's majority populations regard the Nuristanis with ambivalence. Consequently, Nuristan has remained a backwater of development within the country.

Although not technically "tribes," the peoples of Nuristan will sometimes be referred to as "tribes" here, in keeping with the common usage for Pashtun groups of comparable size. The reader should be aware that from the Nuristanis' viewpoint, each "tribe" is an independent people, as separate from each other as the English, Germans, and Dutch.

ETHNICITY AND TRIBES

In Nuristan, every tribe has a name and an autonomous status vis-à-vis the other tribes. An awareness of ethnicity underlies all interpersonal relations in Nuristan. Ethnic identity and clan affiliation are inherited from one's father. Patriarchy and kinship are the cultural foundations of Nuristani society, while autonomous communities are the fundamental units of Nuristani society.

However, ethnicity alone does not explain the complex and sometimes conflicting networks of Nuristani interaction. A short synopsis of the named peoples of Nuristan, grouped by language, follows.

There is no single designation for the seven distinct peoples who speak Kamkata-vari, the major language of Nuristan. Of these, the **Kata** are the most populous people in Nuristan. They extend out from their ancient center of Kantiwa into the upper watersheds of eastern and western Nuristan. Although they are a single ethnicity, the Kata of each valley normally operate independently of each other. They tend to maintain an arrogant attitude toward other Nuristanis. They have strong traditional ties to the national military. The Kata of Bargi Matal district declared themselves an independent Salafi state during the Soviet War, and Salafi clerics are still strong in that district. Insurgents operate in some western Kata areas.

Closely related to the Kata are three minor but separate peoples that long ago migrated into today's Kamdesh district: the **Mumo, Kushto**, and **Binio**. There are two other minor peoples: the **Jamcho**, who came from Jamach in Waygal, and the **Jashi**, who are remnants of the original inhabitants of Nuristan. The communities of the latter three peoples are surrounded by Kom lands, speak the Kom dialect, and are dominated by the Kom politically. Insurgents currently operate out of the highlands of Mumo and Jashi territory.

The **Kom** are the second largest Kamkata-vari-speaking population in Nuristan and are not perceived as being "close" to other Nuristani groups. They have a somewhat bellicose reputation, and they are traditional enemies of the Kata, Kushto, and Sanu. Insurgents operate out of some of the Koms' eastern highlands.

The **Vasi** speak their own language, Vasi-vari, which neighboring Nuristanis cannot understand. They were the keepers of the pre-Islamic religion and have a reputation as being docile. They were supporters of Jamiat-e Islami during the Soviet War.

The **Kalasha** are a group of peoples of diverse origins and languages. Prominent among these are the Kalasha of the Waygal Valley, who themselves are three unrelated peoples: the **Vai**, the **Cima-Nishei**, and the **Vanta**. These three peoples speak the Kalasha-ala language. Many high-ranking military officers have been Waygal-Valley Kalasha. Salafi-oriented insurgents sometimes operate near the Vai communities of Ameshos and Arans.

The **Tregami** are another separate group of Kalasha, with their own language.

The **Sanu** and **Gramsana** are separate Kalasha peoples who, along with the **Ashkun**, speak dialects of a language known as Ashkunu. The Ashkun people are divided among three valleys: Titin, Masegal (Kolatan), and Badzaigal. The Masegal Valley was a Jamiati stronghold during the Soviet war, led by a commander who is a current parliamentary representative.

The **Pashai** are a group of peoples of diverse origins who all speak dialects of the Pashai language. In Nuristan province there are at least three separate Pashai-speaking populations: the **Malil-aw-Mashpa**, the **Chugani**, and the people of the west side of the **Alingar** watershed.

Small populations of **Pashtuns** and **Gujars** have settled in southwestern Nuristan in recent generations. Other highland populations of Pashtuns and Gujars have been gradually expropriating Nuristani lands in the Kunar watershed over the past century. This expansion of Pashtuns and Gujars is the major source of inter-ethnic conflict in the region.

Certain Nuristani peoples have maintained mutually hostile relations over resources and feuds. Communities as a whole defend their water and timber resources. Clans manage and defend their pastureland resources, and they defend themselves through retaliation in kind for any aggression against their members. Retaliation can be stopped through compensation negotiated by mutually acceptable mediators. Within a community, mediators will step in to quell potential violence; but without acceptable mediators (as is often the case between disputants of different ethnic groups), feuds can go on indefinitely.

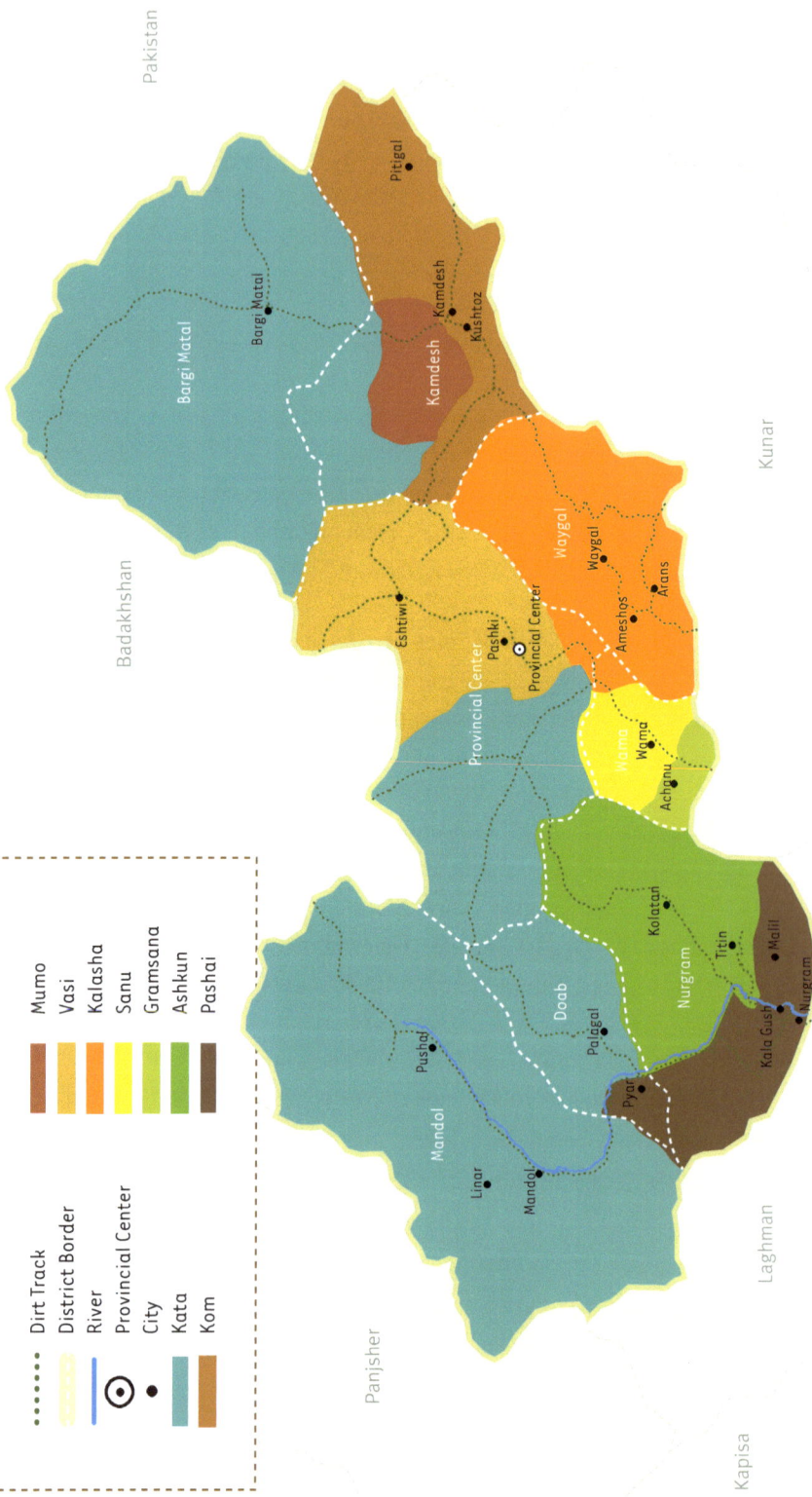

Map 2. Tribal Map of Nuristan

Legend:
- Dirt Track
- District Border
- River
- Provincial Center
- City
- Kata
- Kom
- Mumo
- Vasi
- Kalasha
- Sanu
- Gramsana
- Ashkun
- Pashai

Pakistan

Badakhshan

Kunar

Panjsher

Kapisa

Laghman

Bargi Matal
Pitigal
Kamdesh
Kushtoz
Kamdesh
Waygal
Waygal
Arans
Ameshos
Eshtiwi
Pashki
Provincial Center
Wama
Wama
Achgnu
Kolatan
Titin
Malil
Nurgram
Nurgram
Kala Gush
Pryal
Palagal
Doab
Pushal
Mandol
Mandol
Linar

The peoples of Nuristan are listed by district in Table 5.

How These Groups Govern

Nuristanis manage their internal affairs through traditions of community-level democracy. Decisions affecting the community as a whole are made in open community gatherings, under the informal guidance of community leaders who are called "elders" in the local languages. Within a community, an annually-elected body of men enforces decisions and rules affecting resource management. These men are empowered to levy fines against transgressors. Disputes are settled through mediation and the payment of compensation. Infrastructure is maintained through traditionally-organized work groups that include the entire adult male population.

Men become community leaders by repeatedly displaying their skills as orators, peacemakers, or warriors in response to issues or events that affect the community. In times of crisis over a particular issue, a community council may proclaim one or more men as "elders" over the issue, giving them broad powers within the community. They retain their "eldership" as long as they can maintain their community's backing or until the issue is settled, whereupon they return to their role as ordinary citizens.

During the anti-Soviet war, warrior types from various communities were propelled into "eldership" to lead local insurgencies against the communists. As the Hezbis and Jamiatis co-opted the insurgency in the early 1980s with their steady supply of arms and ammunition, they promoted their own more dogmatic adherents, often clerics, as commanders, to the detriment of moderate traditional leaders. After the war, instead of stepping down, some of these commanders retained their local dictatorial powers through continued backing by their parties and local partisans, and sometimes through the murder of their opponents. By the time ISAF troops had arrived, local leadership in many communities had evolved from democracy into petty theocratic dictatorship.

Table 5. Peoples of Nuristan Province

DISTRICT	NATIONAL NAME	LOCAL NAME	LANGUAGE
Waygal	Tregami	Tregami	Tregami
	Waygali	Kalasha: Vai	Kalasha-ala
	Waygali	Kalasha: Chima-Nishei	Kalasha-ala
	Waygali	Kalasha: Vanta	Kalasha-ala
Wama	Wamai	Gramsana	Ashkunu
		Sanu	Ashkunu
	Kordari	Chugani	Pashai
Provincial Center	Kantozi	Kata: Ktivi	Kata-vari
	Paruni	Vasi	Vasi-vari
Kamdesh	Kamozi	Kom	Kamviri
	Jashi	Jashi	Kamviri
	Binozi	Binio	Kamviri
	Jamjozi	Jamcho	Kamviri
	Kushtozi	Kshto	Kamviri
	Mandagali	Mumo	Mumviri
Bargi Matal	Kantozi	Kata: Landai Sin	Kata-vari
Nurgram	Pasha'i	Pashai	Pashai
	Pashtun	Pakhtun	Pashto
	Gujar	Gujar	Gujari
	Pardesi	Ashkun: Titin	Ashkunu
	Pardesi	Ashkun: Masegal	Ashkunu
Doab	Pardesi	Ashkun: Badzaigal	Ashkunu
	Kantozi	Kata: Kulem	Kata-vari
	Pasha'i	Pashai	Pashai
	Gujar	Gujar	Gujari
Mandol	Kantozi	Kata: Ramgal	Kata-vari

Other Human Networks

- Most important is the informal network of elders who know one another through kin contacts and compatible reputations.

- Important for security is the network of jihadist insurgents, supported through certain mosques and Pakistani jihadist religious schools.

- The so-called "timber mafia" is a multi-ethnic network active in smuggling timber out of eastern Nuristan and Kunar into Pakistan.

- A less visible "gem mafia" smuggles illegally mined gemstones out to the global market, usually through Pakistan.

LANGUAGES

There are five separate but related **Nuristani** languages spoken by some fifteen ethnic groups across Nuristan province. Additionally, the **Pashai** language is spoken in Nurgram and Doab districts of western Nuristan province. Within those districts, **Gujari** is spoken by Gujar settlers.

Most adult Nuristani males and many females speak **Pashto** or **Dari** as second languages. Dari is spoken as a first language in a few westernmost Nuristani villages of Mandol district, close to Dari-speaking Panjsher province. Pashto is spoken as a first language by most of the Kom Nuristani population of the Kunar Valley in the disputed Ghaziabad district, as well as by the Pashtuns in western Nurgram district.

A summary of languages spoken in Nuristan Province appears in Table 6.

RELIGION

Nuristanis are Sunni Muslims of the Hanafi doctrine, like the majority of Muslims in Afghanistan. During the Soviet war, Ikhwani and Salafi operatives, bringing money and conservative teachings from Egypt and

Table 6. Languages of Nuristan Province

LINGUISTIC GROUP	LINGUISTIC NAME	PASHTO NAME	LOCAL NAME	ETHNIC GROUPS	DISTRICTS
Nuristani	Vasi-vari	Paruni	vasi vari	Vasi	Provincial Center
	Kamkata-vari	Kantozi	kata-vari	Kata	Provincial Center, Bargi Matal, Doab, Mandol
		Mandagali	mumviri	Mumo	Kamdesh
		Kamdeshi	kamviri, kshtaviri	Kom, Kushto	
	Ashkunu	Wamai	sanu viri	Sanu	Wama
			gramsana viri	Gramsana	
			ashkunu viri	Ashkun	Nurgram, Doab
	Kalasha-ala	Waygali	vai ala	Vai	Waygal
			nishei ala	Nishei	
	Tregami	Tregami	tregami	Tregami	
Indo-Aryan	Pashai	Pasha'i	pashai	Pashai	Nurgram, Doab, Wama
	Gujari	Gujari	gujari	Gujar	Nurgram, Doab
Iranian	Pashto	Pashto	pakhto	Pashtun	Nurgram
	Persian	Dari	farsi or dari	Kata	Mandol

Saudi Arabia, set up pockets of more radically conservative forms of Islamic worship in some villages of Bargi Matal and Waygal districts.

RELEVANT CULTURAL POINTS – BELIEFS, PREJUDICES, BEHAVIOR

Nuristan is a bastion of patriarchy. Younger persons defer to their elders, and women defer to men.

There are no local taboos aside from the numerous Islamic ones observed in eastern Afghanistan. Among those the most important are: never show your private parts or fart in the presence of locals, and never make sexual remarks in the presence of women.

Islam in Nuristan has become more conservative over the generations, as it falls further under the influence of conservative Pakistani and jihadist mullahs. This has led to a persistent "culture war" between the conservative mullahs and advocates of traditional Nuristani culture. For example, there is a major battle over traditional music and dance, which the mullahs try to ban. Feel privileged if you get to sit in on a Nuristani music and dance party.

Nuristani leaders are keenly competitive, sometimes to the point of becoming sworn enemies. It is important to learn the extent of enmity between local leaders in order to avoid bringing enemies together at meetings.

Greeting rituals are more elaborate in Nuristan than Americans are used to. One always starts by asking about the other's health, followed by the health of the other's family and livestock. Following the local custom, hosts offer their guests tea with sugar and cookies if they come for discussions or a casual visit.

Most communities govern themselves through open gatherings under the informal guidance of elders. Insurgents sometimes try to intimidate those participating in this traditional mode of democracy.

PHOTO BY DAVID KATZ

Chapter 3
Government and Leadership

A fghanistan's centrally-dominated official government is largely ineffective in Nuristan due to transportation difficulties, lack of facilities, and shortages of government personnel. As they have for much of their history, Nuristanis rely on traditional community decision-making and tribal customs for governance. A few areas are under the political influence of powerful clerics.

HOW THE GOVERNMENT OFFICIALLY WORKS

Central Control

Authority and power in Afghanistan are concentrated in the national government in order to counter the power of warlords in the provinces. As such, the provincial government is limited to an advisory role for the central government, while decisions on everything from policy to funding priorities are made in Kabul.

Provincial Government

A governor (*wali*) heads the provincial government and reports to the Independent Directorate for Local Governance (IDLG) located in the Executive Office of the president. A deputy and several staff that oversee provincial government management assist him.

Ministries in Kabul execute their policies and programs through departments located at the provincial level. Ministers, with the approval of the president, appoint provincial directors who manage the departments. The director reports to and receives funds from the ministry in Kabul. The governor does not have budgetary authority over any of these departments, but must approve all expenditures before they are processed by the Department of Finance (*Mustafiat*).

The Provincial Council (PC), the only elected body at the provincial level, plays an advisory role. The PC reports directly to the president and has no budget. Its relevance largely depends on the governor's support and on its members' individual resources and ambition.

The Provincial Development Committee (PDC), including the governor and department heads, is responsible for creating the Provincial Development Plan (PDP) and coordinating with key players on development needs. External players such as the UN, PRT, and interested NGOs also attend meetings.

District and Local Governance

Government at the district level mirrors the provincial government with the *woluswal* (district administrator or sub-governor), police chief, National Directorate of Security officer, clerks, and a small police force. Ministry sub-departments also operate at the district level, but are not present in every district. In 2007, District Development Assemblies

(DDAs) were formed in order to plan, prioritize and coordinate development activities at the district level. Below the district level, the only formal governance structures are the Community Development Councils (CDCs). These CDCs help the Ministry of Rural Rehabilitation and Development (MRRD) manage the National Solidarity Program.

HOW IT ACTUALLY WORKS

Because the official government is weak, most communities still govern themselves as described in Chapter 2 of this handbook. But in communities still under the sway of pro-Hezbi or jihadist clerics, such as Pitigal in Kamdesh district, those trying to adhere to traditional democracy are intimidated by the hooded insurgent thugs who come in the night to enforce the clerics' edicts. Traditional practices of leadership and governance, which have served the Nuristanis well for so long, cannot flourish as long as the jihadist clerics and insurgency are active.

Beyond the governor's immediate circle, the formal structure of Nuristan province is minimally functioning. Road building is a developmental priority, but much of it is on hold due to insurgent activity. The Ministries of Education (MoE), Public Health (MoPH), and Rural Rehabilitation and Development (MRRD) and the Department of Public Works (DoPW) reportedly have active programs in Nuristan, but their profile is minimal. The representatives to the national parliament reportedly have minimal impact in Kabul.

A vacancy in the provincial governor's office during much of 2008 allowed the provincial government to fall into even greater disarray than it had been in before. The government in Nuristan is reported to be minimally functioning, with many governmental personnel moving to Kunar for greater accessibility to Kabul.

Table 7. Key Provincial Governmental Offices

DISTRICT	OFFICE	NAME	ETHNIC GROUP	COMMENTS
Provincial Center	Governor	Jamaluddin Badr	Kata – Bargi Matal	
	Deputy Governor	Haji Abdul Halim	Kata – Ktivi	
	Chief of Police	General Qasim Jugalbullah		
	National Directorate of Security Director	Taza Gul		
	Wolesi Jirga Rep	Haji Dad Mohammad	Ashkun	
	Wolesi Jirga Rep	Hawa Alam Nooristani	Afghan	Married to Wamai
	Meshrano Jirga	Sher Mohammad	Kata	
	Meshrano Jirga	Nurullah	Kata – Ktivi	
	Provincial Council Representative	Munawar Nizami		
Wama	District Administrator	Haji Din Mohammad	Ashkun	
	Provincial Council Representative	Mawlawi Mohammad Gul		
Waygal	District Administrator	Mohammad Osman		
	Provincial Council Representatives	Bibi Zarmina Atiqan Haqdad Khan	Nishei	
Kamdesh	District Administrator	Enayatullah	Kom	
	Provincial Council Representatives	Bibi Narges Gul Alai	Kom	
Bargi Matal	District Administrator	Malawi Mohammad Ishmael	Kata	
	Provincial Council Representative	Rahmatullah Rashidi	Kata	
Nurgram	District Administrator	Mohammad Ali	Pasai-Pashagar	
	Provincial Council Representative			
Doab	District Administrator	Qari Daud		
	Provincial Council Representative	Mawlawi Taj Mohammad		
Mandol	District Administrator	Abdul Qadeer		
	Provincial Council Representative			

Most Nuristanis would like to see the insurgency ended, but beyond that they are not overly troubled by the lack of central government institutions. They do, however, want schools with trained teachers and clinics with doctors and nurses.

SECURITY FORCES

Security is mostly occupied with anti-government insurgents, but it is largely ineffective in preventing them from setting up temporary roadblocks to harass the local travelling population. Police presence and training in the province is minimal. The ANA maintains an artillery unit stationed at FOB Kala Gush, where they are mentored by the USMC. Other units are stationed with ISAF personnel at outposts in Kamdesh district.

POLITICAL PARTIES AND ELECTIONS

Electoral political parties are largely irrelevant in Nuristan. Nuristan is a kinship-based society, and a Nuristani will normally vote for his closest relative in elections.

2009 ELECTIONS

Presidential and Provincial Council elections are scheduled to take place on 20 August 2009. When President Karzai's term expired in May, he began serving as a caretaker president until elections could be held. Candidates for president filed in May, but few national contenders emerged, as President Karzai persuaded many of his rivals not to challenge him. In terms of security, Afghan National Security

Forces (ANSF) will be extensively involved in the elections, recruiting 23,000 police and soldiers for the event. The security of the elections represents a potential key moment for the summer fighting season between Taliban and ANSF/ISAF troops. After the elections, changes in the Afghan government will involve new senior appointments, including new ministers and governors. Late 2009 and 2010 will be a key period for these new officials to leverage their public mandate and expanded international assistance to deliver more accountable and credible governance to the Afghan people.

A more detailed update on elections is included in the back folder of your book or can be downloaded at *www.idsinternational.net/ afpakbooks*. The pre-elections update goes into the elections process in greater detail and the post-election update summarizes the results and implications.

LEADER PROFILES

Government/Political Leaders

Jamaluddin Badr, Governor: Jamaluddin was appointed Nuristan's governor on 25 November 2008. He was born around 1975, and left his home at about age 10 to be educated at a Peshawar, Pakistan madrassa (Jam-e Asadya) for about eight years. He later received his university degree in Islamic studies at Medina City, Saudi Arabia. He speaks Dari, Pashto, Arabic, Persian, Urdu, and limited English. Jamaluddin was previously an political officer for the Ministry of Foreign Affairs working on Middle East issues. He was chief of the Bargi Matal Ulama Council from 2003-2004.

Jamaluddin is reportedly close to the Dawat-e Islami political party. He is also known to be close to former classmate and current Bargi Matal district administrator, Ishmael.

Haji "Ma'mur" Abdul Halim, Deputy Governor: He has held the same position under previous governors. In November 2006 he was charged with resolving the Kamdesh-Kushtoz dispute. Halim is a cousin of former governor Tamim Nuristani, from Kantiwa. He was formerly associated with HIG, and suspicions remain that he may retain those links.

Dr. Ahmad Yusuf Nuristani, Governor of Herat Province: A Kalasha from Nisheigram, he attended Rahman Baba boarding school in Kabul, then Kabul University. He continued his studies in the US and received a PhD from the University of Arizona, Tucson. Yusuf is the highest-ranking Nuristani in the Afghan government, having served as First Deputy Minister of Defense, Minister of Environment, and also as spokesman for President Karzai. In addition to Dari, Pashto, English, and Urdu, he is fluent in Kalasha-ala, his native language, and Kata-vari. He stays involved in Nuristani affairs although his official responsibilities make it difficult for him to find the time to travel to the province. He is a vigorous advocate for Nuristan with the national government and international community.

During the Soviet occupation, he affiliated with the Mahaz-e Milli of Pir Gailani. He also worked at the American Center in Peshawar, Pakistan. In the 1990s he was affiliated with German NGOs working in the education sector. (Phone: 0799-888-877; E-mail: *ahmad-nuristani@yahoo.com*)

Ethnic Leaders

Mullah Abdullah Sher Gul, Former Governor: A Vasi (Paruni) from
Deva village, Sher Gul was governor from 2002-2005. A mullah
from Dewa village in Parun, he was active in the JI during the jihad.
Described as an old-fashioned, conservative Wahhabi cleric, he led
the effort to organize Nuristan's religious leaders to oppose the
Taliban. During his tenure as governor he was not active in development and reconstruction. Karzai sacked him in February 2005,
replacing him with Tamim Nuristani. He reportedly retains influence
with the religious leaders in the province. In the 2004 presidential
elections, he supported Qanuni over Karzai.

**Wakil Dad Mohammad, Representative (wakil) to the Peoples'
Assembly:** A prominent JI commander during the jihad, he continued
to head a militia affiliated with Nangarhar strongman Hazrat Ali until
2004. Although illiterate, he represents Nuristan in the Wolesi Jirga.

Although he was demobilized as a militia commander in November
2004, he is believed to retain caches of weapons, and is rumored to
have surface-to-air missiles. After surrendering most of his weapons,
he became upset and sent a letter to the US government stating that,
since there were many anti-government groups operating in his area,
if the ANA was not going to defeat them, then he should be given back
his weapons so he could do it.

He has been described as a shrewd politician but ineffectual as a
wakil (member of parliament). He is an Ashkun from Kolatan.

Both Nuristani representatives in the Wolesi Jirga, Dad Mohammad
and Hawa Alam, have ties to Ashkun: Dad Mohammad is from
Kulatan and Hawa Alam's husband is from Wama district. (Phone:
0700-066-8982)

Gul Mohammad Khan, Woluswal: A respected leader of the Kom, he was principal of the Kamdesh school when the Soviet war began. He supported the local jihad, later allying with Sayyaf's party. He has served as woluswal in Kamdesh and Bargi Matal districts. He has close ties with Kom Hezbis, but is pro-government.

Anti-Government Leaders

Haji Ghafur: A major HIG insurgent in Nuristan, he has eluded capture and reportedly hides out in Shuk in Doab district and Kust in Wama district. A Kata from Kantiwa, Ghafur is a cousin of both Deputy Governor Abdul Halim and former Governor Tamim.

Mullah Sadiq: A Kom from Upper Kamdesh, Sadiq is a former HIG commander of Kamdesh and a major target of ISAF. To date he has eluded capture.

A boy and his father prepare a plow. Nuristanis live off subsistence farming and are content in their self-sufficiency. They have developed cooperative networks to efficiently use pastureland, arable land, and water resources.

PHOTO BY DAVID KATZ

Chapter 4
The Economy

The people of Nuristan live at a subsistence level, with an economy based on a mixture of agriculture, tree crops, and livestock. The mountainous environment supports these economic pursuits adequately to maintain the present population. Any accumulation of wealth derived from this traditional economy is contained and redistributed within Nuristan or spent on consumer items; there is very little reinvestment in capital improvements that could raise the standard of living.

POLITICAL ECONOMY

Over the centuries, Nuristanis have developed cooperative networks to efficiently use pastureland, arable land, and water resources. These networks are not easily transformable into modern models of cooperatives for production and marketing, being firmly based in traditional methods and intertwined with tribal and other relationships. Nuristanis are content in their self-sufficiency and are not anxious to alter these networks.

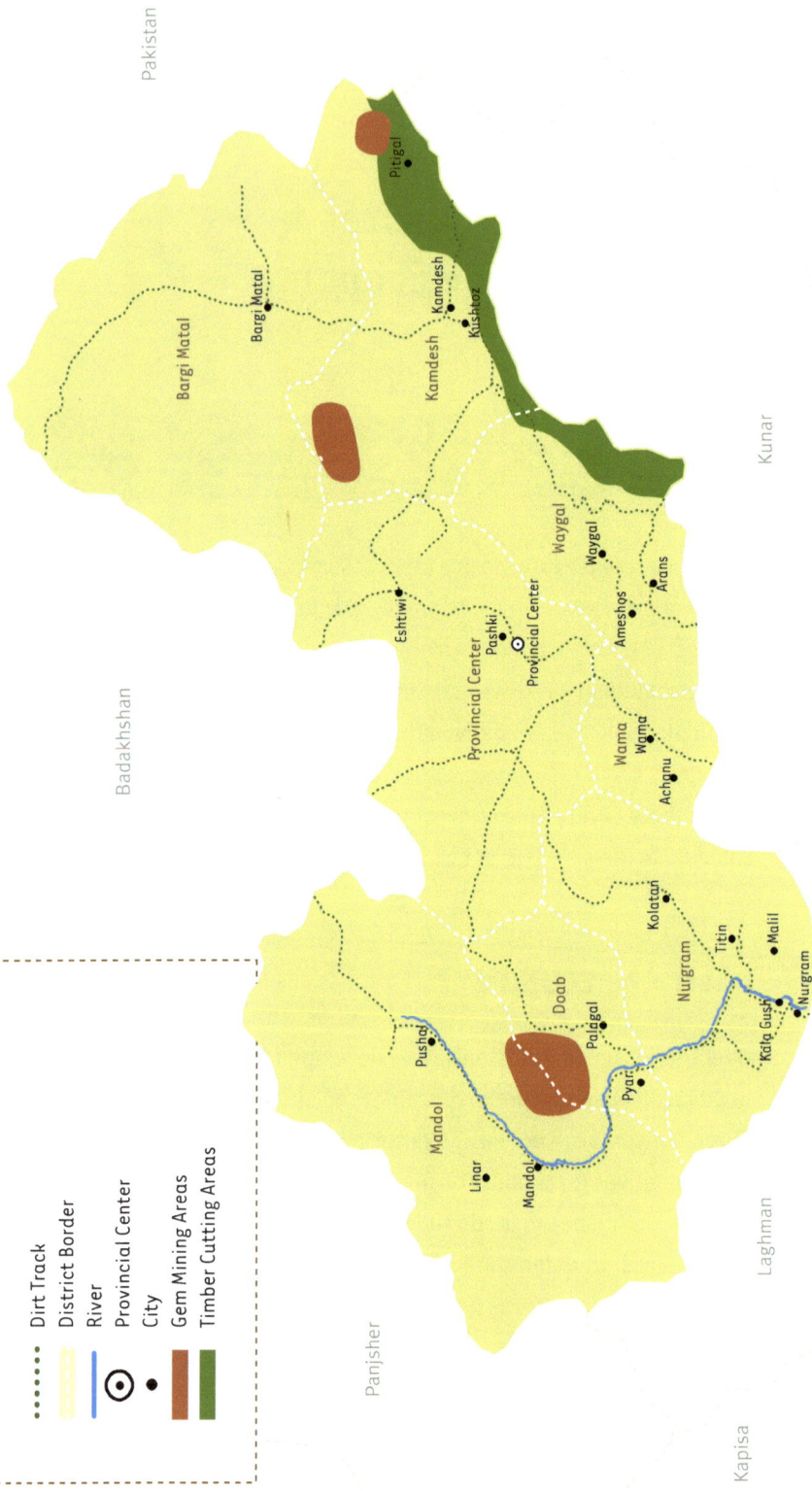

Map 3. Economic Map of Nuristan

Legend:
- Dirt Track
- District Border
- River
- Provincial Center
- City
- Gem Mining Areas
- Timber Cutting Areas

Labels on map:

Pakistan

Badakhshan

Kunar

Panjsher

Kapisa

Laghman

Pitigal

Bargi Matal

Bargi Matal

Kamdesh

Kamdesh

Kushtoz

Waygal

Waygal

Ameshos

Arans

Eshtiwi

Pashki

Provincial Center

Provincial Center

Wama

Wama

Achgnu

Kolatan

Nurgram

Titin

Malil

Nurgram

Kata Gus

Doab

Palagal

Pyar

Pushal

Mandol

Mandol

Linar

Nuristan produces a few commodities sold in global and regional markets. Traditional exports to surrounding regions include walnuts, apricot seeds, pine nuts, goats, clarified butter, morel mushrooms, cumin, and animal hides. International donor agencies hope to develop the economic potential of these commodities as soon as security becomes available in the province.

Significant amounts of cash are currently flowing into Nuristan's economy from development projects, such as labor-intensive US DoD Commander's Emergency Response Program (CERP) road programs and the USAID Alternative Development Program/Eastern Region (ADP/ER). Such cash infusions are driving the traditional economy toward consumerism and closer ties with the national economy.

INFRASTRUCTURE

Transportation

There are extremely few roads, all of which are unpaved and subject to closure from flooding in the summer and avalanches in the winter. An aggressive road-building program is underway, with the USACE funding major roads to connect district centers, and CERP funds for important spur routes. However, progress is greatly impeded by insurgents and poor management.

Electricity

The National Risk and Vulnerability Assessment 2005 asserts that 62 percent of Nuristani households have access to electricity, although knowledgeable observers believe that estimate is high. Electricity has just started to appear in Nuristan's villages in the past few years through community micro-hydroelectric generating systems. CERP funds are responsible for some of these, but many are the result of private investment. Otherwise, most of Nuristan remains without electricity and without potential connection to a national power grid.

Communications

Cellular phone service in now available in limited areas of Nuristan, and new towers are being installed regularly. There are no land-line phones. ISAF has been installing CODAN radios at police offices in district centers to allow communication with their provincial headquarters.

KEY SECTORS

Two natural resources distributed throughout much of Nuristan, timber and gemstones, provide a significant boost to the region's economy. These resources have been exploited and sold on regional and global markets over the past few decades, with mixed benefits to a portion of the population. Tree crops of walnuts and fruit have been traditional regional exports and are now targeted for development for wider distribution.

Animal Products

Half the subsistence economy of Nuristan depends on an indigenous dairy industry that produces cheese, butter, ghee, and curds. These are consumed regularly in every Nuristani household. The populations surrounding Nuristan also covet and occasionally buy these goods from Nuristanis. Goats and cattle, kept in a roughly five-to-one ratio, provide both milk for dairying and meat for local consumption. An active export trade in animal hides through Afghan middlemen has existed throughout local memory.

Because of Nuristan's isolation, its exports, regardless of commodity, must go through external Afghan or Panjsheri middlemen to get to their ultimate markets. Most of the profits from these Nuristani products accrue to the middlemen. This system discourages Nuristanis from setting up their own profitable markets directly with consumers.

Timber

Nuristan encompasses a major portion of Afghanistan's timber reserves. Deodar cedar is the primary timber commodity, with pine, fir, and spruce being less exploited. Little commercial exploitation of Nuristan's forests occurred before the Soviet-Afghan war because of the difficult terrain. When hostilities ceased after the fall of the communists, timber merchants from Pakistan aggressively moved into eastern Nuristan. They bulldozed roads into some valleys to more easily remove the cut timber, which is transported to Pakistan and sold as far away as the Arab Gulf states. They have made large profits on this trade, and the looting of Afghanistan's timber resources by Pakistanis in collusion with certain locals engenders much of the hostility found along Afghanistan's eastern frontier.

The central government has banned all logging activity. Special permits are required to haul timber, but these regulations are for the most part unenforced. Although stricter enforcement of the ban would protect a valuable resource, it would also interrupt one of the few activities that brings in any outside source of income, as well as engender hostility toward the central government.

Gemstones and Minerals

Since the late 1960s Nuristanis have become aware that their region contains significant deposits of marketable, high quality gemstones. Most important is tourmaline, followed by kunzite, aquamarine, spodumene, beryl, and garnet. Additionally, there are reported deposits of emerald and peridot. Most of the gem deposits are in remote, mountainous areas, and some are accessible for only a few months of the year due to Afghanistan's hard winters. Most of Nuristan's presumed mineral resources have not been exploited; only about 500 low-wage miners work on a daily basis in Nuristan.

Tree Crops

Tree crops provide an important portion of the Nuristanis' diet. Fruits include mulberries, apricots, pomegranates, grapes, apples, figs, jujubes, pears, peaches, and persimmons. Nut crops include walnuts, almonds, pine nuts, hazelnuts, and edible apricot seeds. Dried mulberries and apricots also are produced in surplus in some communities. Walnut production was a major source of income for the Nuristanis before the Soviet-Afghan war, but market production of walnuts declined in the war's aftermath. Development projects are just beginning to upgrade Nuristan's horticultural potential.

TRENDS AND RELEVANT ISSUES FOR TODAY

Development agencies are ready to move in with forestry, orchard development, and educational projects. Securing the province for unimpeded development is a top priority. This entails protecting development personnel as well as the local populace from acts of terrorism and criminality of the kinds routinely perpetrated in Kamdesh and Doab districts today.

Timber smuggling and illegal gemstone mining are persistent problems. Smugglers and illegal miners sometimes cooperate with insurgents in their common goal of resisting the government, especially in Mandol and Doab districts.

Nuristan's terrain and isolation have hindered reconstruction projects. Increased insurgent presence has halted NGO activity. The PRT is the primary source of reconstruction efforts in Nuristan.

PHOTO BY STAFF SGT. BRANDON AIRD

Chapter 5
International Organizations and Reconstruction Activities

Nuristanis regard the presence of ISAF troops with mixed feelings. Most of the population supports ISAF's presence as a deterrent to insurgents, although many residents of insurgent-controlled areas feel that ISAF troops are not doing enough to protect them. Many mullahs make propaganda against the presence of "infidel" foreigners in their region, using arguments that sway their more impressionable parishioners.

Geographical isolation and continued insurgent activity combine to limit IO and NGO activity in Nuristan. The organizations listed in Table 9 have been active in Nuristan in the past and have indicated an intention to continue working in the province. Some are still represented in the province by Afghan employees. However, with the exception of the PRT, there were no foreign assistance workers based in the province at the time of this writing (June 2009).

KEY RECONSTRUCTION ACTIVITIES

Assistance agencies are ready to move into Nuristan with planned assistance programs, but because the insurgency has been targeting reconstruction and development projects there, most international NGO activities have been temporarily halted.

Infrastructure

Roads: A lack of all-weather roads connecting key areas of the province is a major impediment to governance and economic development. Local contractors are carrying out several road construction projects with international (USACE, USAID, PRT, UNOPS) and ministerial (MRRD, MoPW) funding. The roads are designed to connect the major Nuristani valleys to the Kabul-Torkham Highway, as well as to connect the western and eastern valleys with the central valley and the provincial center in the Parun Valley. Amerifa has been the major contractor for roads in Nuristan. Security and other problems have slowed construction progress.

Power: Local entrepreneurs and NGOs have built community hydropower projects in a few villages since the mid 1990s. Insurgents destroyed a generator for Kamdesh village shortly after it was put in service in 2004, but it was subsequently rebuilt. The NGO AfghanAid carried out some of these small-scale construction projects, and the USACE is funding more micro-hydropower projects.

Education

Education Indicators: Nuristanis understand the need for education to compete in today's marketplace. In addition to basic education for children, vocational training is in demand. However, educational facilities of all types are inadequate. Insurgent activities hamper more rapid construction of educational facilities.

The Nuristani and Pashai languages remain unwritten. Measures of literacy are for Pashto or Dari, spoken as second languages by many Nuristanis. The overall literacy rate in those languages is estimated at 25 percent in Nuristan. However, while nearly one-third of men are literate (31 percent), this is true for only around one-fifth of women (19 percent). The male population aged between 15 and 24 is less literate than the general male population, with 25 percent literacy. For women in the same age group, the figure shows an even greater decrease in the literacy rate to just nine percent. The Pashtun population in the province has particularly low levels of literacy, with 4.2 percent of men and no women able to read and write.

Education Infrastructure: Nuristan has about 150 schools, 20 in dedicated buildings and the rest in makeshift quarters. Due to both basic need and as a COIN strategy, the Ministry of Education has made Nuristan a priority, and new schools are being built; but again, construction has been slowed by insurgent activity. The Indian government was supporting school construction in 2007, and USAID and the PRT have continuing programs.

Healthcare

Health Indicators: Most Nuristanis do not have access to professional health care. Instead, 92 percent of Nuristanis consult traditional healers for their healthcare needs. According to the Swedish Committee for Afghanistan (SCA), the most common medical issues in the province are tuberculosis, acute respiratory infection, diarrhea, worm infestations, and typhoid. The typical Nuristani household has roughly nine members per family. Infant mortality is higher than Afghanistan's national average at 16.5 percent, with one in four children dying before the age of five. It is common for mothers to die in childbirth. Without a professional healthcare system, it is difficult to judge whether the situation is improving.

Table 8. Primary and Secondary Education

	SCHOOLS		STUDENTS		TEACHERS	
	Boys	Girls	Boys	Girls	Male	Female
Primary	90	38	15,551	9,165	N/A	N/A
Secondary	12	2	638	38	N/A	N/A
TOTAL	102	40	16,189	9,203	917	78
	142		25,392		995	

Health Infrastructure: Recently, health-care facilities have had a modest expansion in Nuristan to six Comprehensive Health Clinics and nine Basic Health Centers.

The following types of facilities are found in the province:

Basic Health Center (BHC): Serves a population up to 30,000 people. Outpatient care only, similar to Level I military care. Basic OB/GYN, routine immunizations, childhood diseases, treatment of malaria, TB, and care for mental health patients and disabled patients.

Comprehensive Health Clinic (CHC): Serves a population up to 60,000 people. Similar to Level II military care. Limited inpatient care, basic laboratory, severe childhood illnesses, and malaria. Staffed with male and female doctors, nurses, midwives, lab, and pharmacy techs.

There is no District/Provincial Level Hospital in Nuristan to provide any higher level of care. The nearest such facility is in Jalalabad.

Table 9. Health Services (hospitals and clinics by district)

NAME	DISTRICT	TOWN	TYPE
Parun Health Clinic	Provincial Center	Pashki	BHC
PMS	Wama	Wama	CHC
Wama Basic Health Center	Wama	Achanu	BHC
Kordar Comprehensive Health Center	Wama	Kordar	CHC
Waygal Basic Health Center	Waygal	Waygal	BHC
Kamdesh Clinic	Kamdesh	Ormol	CHC
Ormol Kamdesh Clinic	Kamdesh	Ormol	BHC
Bargi Matal Comprehensive Health Center	Bargi Matal	Bargi Matal	CHC
Clinic related to Hamza Hostel School	Bargi Matal	Shudgul	BHC
Basic Health Center	Bargi Matal	Afsay	BHC
Nangarach Basic Health Center	Nurgram	Nangarach	BHC
Doab Comprehensive Health Center	Doab	N/A	BHC
Doab Comprehensive Health Center	Doab	N/A	CHC
Doab Health clinic	Doab	N/A	CHC
Mandol Clinic	Mandol	Mandol	BHC

Source: MRRD Provincial Development Plan Nuristan (2007)

Agriculture

Assistance in this area must collaborative, and care must be taken not to condescend. USAID's Alternative Development Program/Eastern Region (ADP/ER) set up a Perennial Horticulture Program in Nuristan in 2007. After a successful trial planting of 32 hectares of fruit and nut trees in the Waygal and Parun Valleys, 500 hectares of orchards were proposed to be planted in all districts except Bargi Matal during 2008.

PROVINCIAL RECONSTRUCTION TEAM

The PRT was set up in 2006 in collaboration with the provincial government. The PRT in Nuristan consists of a military team and three US government civilian agencies. The military side, consists of a Civil Affairs (CA) team, public affairs team, engineers, and support elements. The civilian side consists of representatives from the US Agency for International Development (USAID), US Department of State (DoS), and US Department of Agriculture (USDA). Together with the maneuver units that have been assigned to the province, the PRT has spent CERP funds on projects desired by Nuristanis and essential to development. USAID provides funding for a variety of projects, including roads, schools and clinics, micro-hydro power, irrigation canals, fruit and nut orchards, training and mentoring for officials and civil servants, mining, and construction of provincial administrative buildings. The PRT has attempted to coordinate these activities among the units and with the Provincial Development Council whenever possible.

The PRT in Nuristan is currently located at Kala Gush in Nurgram district. There are plans to move the PRT to the provincial center in the Parun Valley, but the continuing difficulty of road access to Parun has delayed the move.

Table 10. PRT and Other USG Agencies

AGENCY	CONTACT	COMMENTS
PRT Commander	CDR George Perez *george.perez@afghan.swa. army.mil*	
PRT Dept of State Rep.	Gregory Phillips *nuristanenvoy@gmail.com*	
PRT USDA Rep.	Danny Markus *dgmarkus@hotmail.com*	
PRT USAID Rep.	Kathrin Lauer *Nuristanusaid@gmail.com*	
ANP Police Training Team		Located at Kala Gush

NATIONAL SOLIDARITY PROGRAM

Several small-scale development projects, such as irrigation and road works, have been carried out under the National Solidarity Program. Most such projects were implemented in relatively secure areas of western and central Nuristan.

Table 11. IOs and NGOs in Nuristan

NAME	CONTACT	ACTIVITY	LOCATION
AfghanAid	**Director in Jalalabad:** Nur Mohammad Najib **Nuristan Provincial Program Manager:** Najibullah Rahmani **Managing Director:** Ms Anne Johnson **In Kabul:** Hs. 94, Hesa-i-Do, Main Rd, Karte Parwan, Kabul (PO Box 6066) **Ph:** 0799-310-498, 0799-310-497, 0799-307-335, 0088-216-8444-4222 **Fax:** 0044-207-255-3344 **Email:** *md@afghanaid.org.uk, melanie@afghanaid.org.uk* **Web:** *www.afghanaid.org.uk*	Livestock, NSP, road rehabilitation, village hydropower, small construction	Kamdesh, Bargi Matal
Afghan Builders Consortium (ABC)	Taj Mohammad, Director **Ph:** 0799-568-002, 0700-224-888 **E-mail:** *ccso.af@gmail.com, ccso_afg@yahoo.com*	Road construction	
Amerifa	Dr. Sayed Noorullah Jalili, President **Ph:** 0799-323-947, 0700-163-292, 0752-004-595 **Thuraya:** 00 882 162 129 4201 Obaidurahman Baha, Chief, Security, Kala Gush **Ph:** 0088-216-211-97074	Major road construction	
BEFA	Nur Mohammad Najib, Director, Jalalabad	Vocational and governmental training	Office in Parun

NAME	CONTACT	ACTIVITY	LOCATION
IMC	N/A	Public health-care	
Mission d'Aide au Développement des Economies Rurales en Afghanistan (MADERA)	N/A	Livestock, NSP, engineering, forest protection.	Kamdesh
Reconstruction Agency of Hindukush (RAH)	Engineer Abdul Khalil Latif, Director **Ph:** 0700 602 610, 0756003439 **Email:** khalil_latif@hotmail.co.uk		
Swedish Committee for Afghanistan (SCA)	N/A	Public health care (currently replaced by IMC for health-care clinics)	All districts
UNOPS	N/A	Logistics	Office in Parun
Saudi-funded religious schools	N/A	Education	Bargi Matal District

Source: UNAMA and others

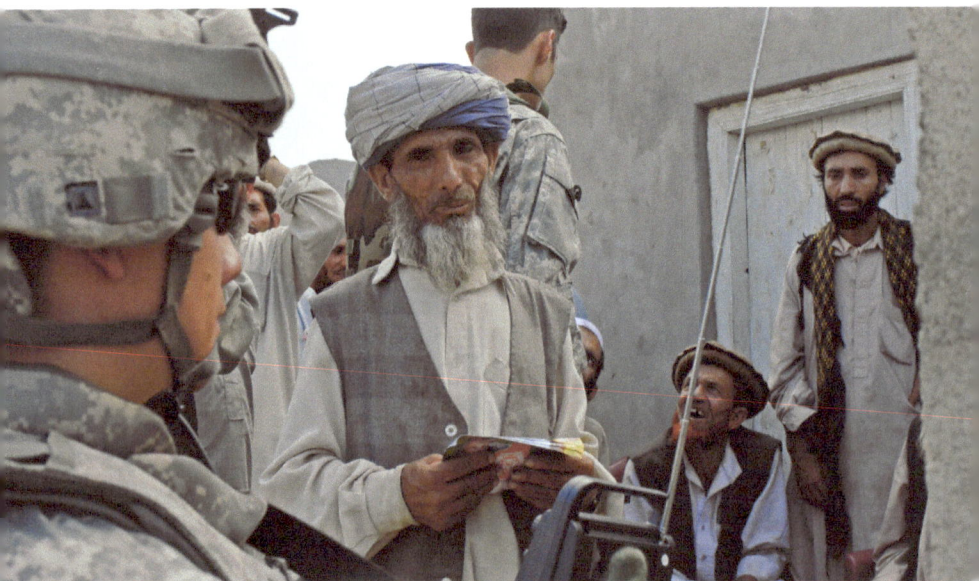

Soldiers hand out radios to villagers of Nengaresh. Radios are the most prevalent source of non-local news among Nuristanis. However, the most trusted news still travels by word of mouth, often exchanged at the mosque after prayers.

PHOTO BY STAFF SGT. ADORA MEDINA

Chapter 6
Information and Influence

nformation still travels mostly by word of mouth in Nuristan. "What's the word?" is always asked of newly arrived acquaintances, and the "word" spreads quite quickly across the region. Influence comes mainly from mullahs in their mosques and elders at community councils or in daily informal conversation.

MEDIA

Because of Nuristan's mountainous remoteness, modern real-time media – except for short-wave radio – are inaccessible to most of the population. Many households have radios and cassette players; very few have televisions, which they use to watch videocassettes; and even fewer have satellite dishes. Radios are the major source of non-local news, with BBC being the most popular source, followed by VOA and regional broadcasts from Afghanistan and Pakistan. Cassettes of regional pop singers are very popular, as are videos of current Indian films.

FOB Naray has set up a local radio station, Zala FM, with a repeater located near Kamdesh. A local radio station aimed at a Nuristani audience also broadcasts out of PRT Kala Gush at 90.0 FM.

The ISAF-published biweekly newspaper *Sada-e Azadi* contains reports from eastern Nuristan. Daily newspapers from Pakistan and Jalalabad occasionally get carried to Nuristan, but in general print media has little influence in Nuristan.

INFORMATION SHARING NETWORKS

Mosques are major forums for information exchange. In every village most men gather at their local mosque to pray five times a day. After prayers they often remain to discuss current affairs.

At Friday noon services in the mosques, mullahs preach sermons, often laced with derogatory references to the "infidels." In mosques where the mullahs support the insurgents, "infidels" are singled out for particular hatred. Some such mullahs, such as Mullah Sadiq of Kamdesh, circulate nasty anti-ISAF hate cassettes through Nuristan's anti-ISAF mosques. A few offer shelter to insurgents, like Mullah Husein in Upper Pitigal who openly harbored anti-government insurgents from Pakistan before his demise in 2007.

Anti-ISAF operatives sometimes circulate so-called "night-letters" in the villages, marking individual government supporters for death if they do not "repent" and support the jihadists. Insurgents in the field use hand-held radios to communicate over wide stretches of highland terrain.

Polling Information

Polling data from most of Nuristan's remote communities is not available, and broad-population statistical data from Nuristan generally remains unreliable. Because information travels mainly by word of mouth, attending social gatherings (such as community councils or receptions for visiting dignitaries) is a good way to find out local issues. Hosting dinners for local leaders is also an appreciated way to find out what they are thinking.

Village councils also serve as forums for information exchange in the process of making community-level decisions. Periodic meetings of ISAF personnel with Nuristani leaders have been successful in sharing information and building trust.

Themes and Perceptions

The insurgency and other local conflicts are major topics of conversation.

A major subtext in today's discourse has to do with "infidels." The presence of "infidel" forces in Nuristan provokes much controversy and discussion, even if a majority of the population supports their mission.

The majority of Nuristanis want rapid development and are impatient with the interruptions caused by insurgents and bureaucratic delays. Encouraging signs of cooperation have emerged out of talks between elders from eastern Nuristan and ISAF soldiers based at Naray in Kunar.

The Nuristan PRT meets with local elders to discuss their concerns. The insurgency, inter-community disputes, and the encroachment of Nuristani land and resources by Gujars and Pashtuns combine to make security the number one issue for Nuristanis.

PHOTO BY DAVID KATZ

Chapter 7
Big Issues

SECURITY

Security is the major issue in Nuristan today. Three types of conflict
pose problems: the jihadist insurgency, inter-community disputes,
and violations of Nuristani lands and resources by intruders.

Hezb-e Islami and Other Jihadists

Nuristan offers the insurgency supply routes from Pakistan, and the
difficult terrain is ideal for sanctuary. The Hezbi insurgency is active
in Kamdesh and Doab districts, along with Taliban operatives in
Mandol district. Remnant Salafi insurgents are active in the villages
of Ameshoz and Arans in Waygal district. Al-Qaeda appears to be
playing an increasing role in insurgent activity in the area and may
be building ties with Hezbi, which in the past viewed al-Qaeda as too
extreme. The movement plays on the political naiveté of many young
Nuristanis from remote villages, equating the US military presence
with that of the "infidel" Soviets.

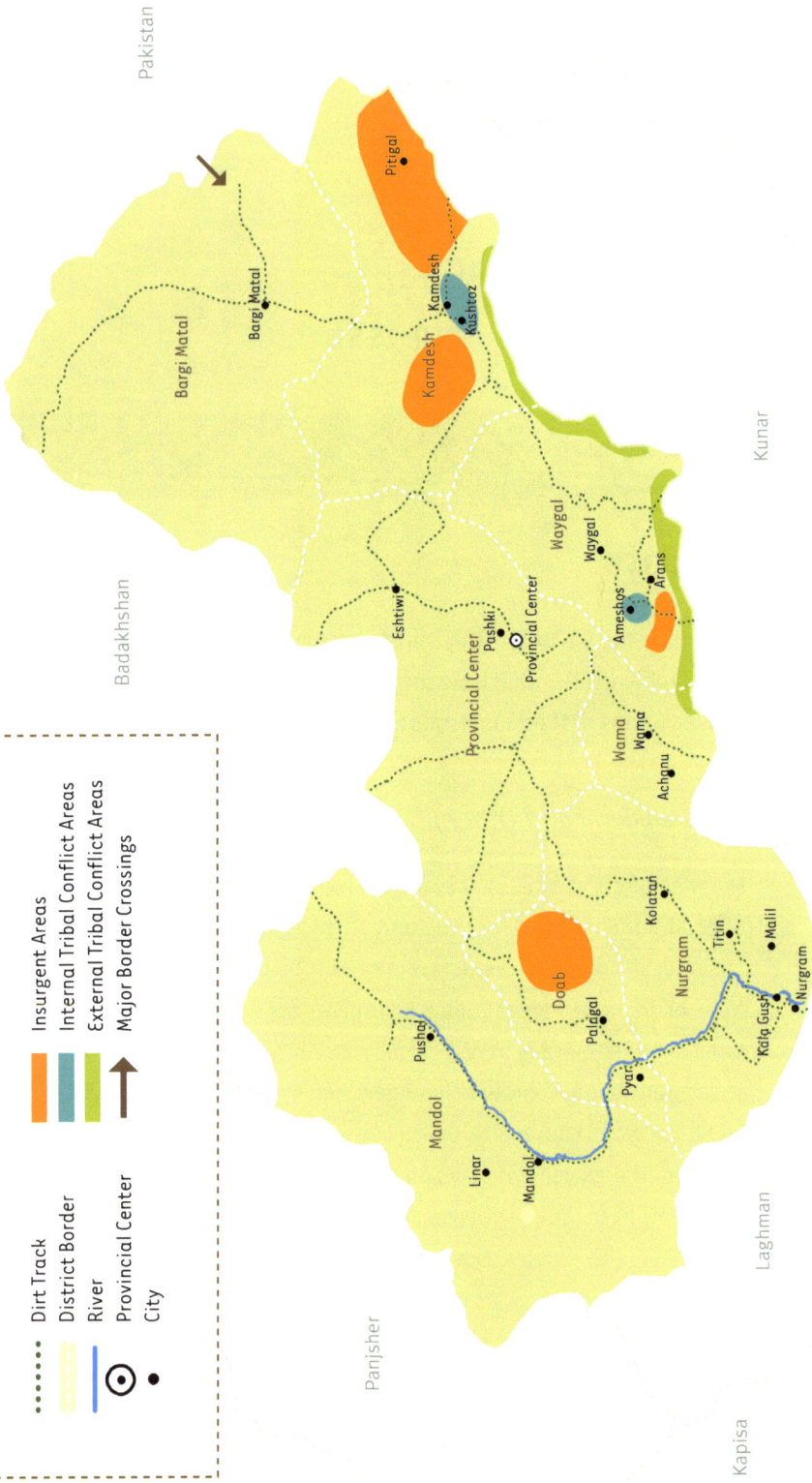

Map 4. Conflict Map of Nuristan

Legend:
- Dirt Track
- District Border
- River
- Provincial Center
- City

- Insurgent Areas
- Internal Tribal Conflict Areas
- External Tribal Conflict Areas
- Major Border Crossings

Surrounding regions: Pakistan, Badakhshan, Kunar, Laghman, Kapisa, Panjsher

Locations: Bargi Matal, Pitigal, Kamdesh, Kushtoz, Eshtiwi, Pashki, Provincial Center, Waygal, Arans, Ameshos, Wama, Achanu, Doab, Kolatan, Nurgram, Titin, Malil, Nurgram, Kotg Gus, Palagal, Pyat, Pushal, Mandol, Linar, Mandol

The insurgents target local residents, development projects, and ISAF soldiers, inflicting numerous casualties. International NGOs and UN agencies have halted operations in Nuristan until security improves. This absence has had some adverse effects on the insurgency, as many locals rightfully blame it for the loss of jobs, funding, and development that would have come with international assistance. However, the longer the international community is absent, the more the locals will accustom themselves to living with the insurgents.

Inter-Community Disputes

In addition to the jihadist insurgency, the inter-community disputes between Kamdesh and Kushtoz in Kamdesh district, between Waygal village and Arans in Waygal district, and between Pyar and Junia in Doab district have also disrupted development projects. Recently, Nuristan's governor settled the latter dispute, and his deputy governor is actively trying to mediate the difficult dispute between Kamdesh and Kushtoz. The jihadists exploit inter-community conflicts. The Hezbis in Kamdesh have aggravated the Kamdesh-Kushtoz conflict by planting mines to kill and maim Kamdeshis, making it look as if the Kushtozis had planted them.

Violations of Lands and Resources

The gradual, long-standing encroachment by Gujars and Pashtuns into Nuristani land along the province's southern border continues to provoke conflict. In addition, robbers and illegal gemstone miners in Mandol and Doab districts reportedly maintain a loose anti-government alliance with local insurgents.

Map 3 shows conflict zones in Nuristan. Insurgent areas are defined as areas where insurgents can operate at will, find safe haven, and exercise influence over the local population. Ethnic-conflict areas are places where land and other disputes periodically cause inter-community violence.

Security has steadily deteriorated in most districts of Nuristan. In Waygal district, contacts between ISAF and insurgents escalated in July 2008, resulting in casualties on both sides. Retaliatory airstrikes killed local friendly civilians, prompting village elders from the district to request that ISAF cease operations there. Reaction to the attacks in Waygal prompted shutdowns of road construction and development projects throughout the province.

Related to the overall security situation are the following continuing issues.

BAD EFFECTS FROM BAD INTELLIGENCE

Insurgent supporters or unscrupulous individuals who pass themselves off as local leaders continue to lie to ISAF personnel. Such individuals seek monetary gain and to provide disinformation about their enemies. One witness explained,

"[ISAF personnel] are dealing with [name deleted] from Upper Pitigal. His sons are insurgents fighting coalition forces. Then he comes down and says he is the shura leader of Pitigal. Lower Pitigal guys who support coalition forces and support the government are voiceless."

Whenever ISAF personnel deal with or appear to support such individuals, they demoralize the non-benefitting population that supports them. ISAF needs to understand who its real friends are and to pay better attention to them.

BAD OFFICIAL MAPS

The attack on ISAF troops near Want in Waygal district on 13 July 2008 highlighted the problem of misdrawn borders and bad nomenclature on the "official" maps (see this handbook, p. 3). The attack was widely reported as having occurred at "Wanat" in "Kunar province," although a few reporters cited the official GIRoA statement that the attack took place in Nuristan. The confusion in such reports prompted HTS at Ft. Leavenworth to issue a cautionary report on map reliability. The unreliability of the boundaries and nomenclature on AIMS maps needs to be reiterated.

GOVERNANCE

Governance in Nuristan has always been problematic because of the difficult terrain and the remoteness of most communities. Previous regimes maintained minimal governance, relying largely on the Nuristani communities to govern themselves in their traditional manner. Currently, most Nuristanis support the national government in principal but are waiting to see how it benefits them. Effective governance in Nuristan is hampered by the lack of roads connecting the provincial center with the district centers, lack of buildings to house governmental offices and personnel, lack of qualified personnel willing to serve in Nuristan, and poorly coordinated planning. Until these problems are overcome and benefits from governmental programs begin to reach the population, most Nuristanis will remain largely aloof toward the national government and will continue to govern themselves as always.

During 2007-08 FOB Naray implemented a "100-man shura" in Kamdesh district in an attempt to connect with the locals. At least one local witness believes that, without adequate follow-up, this well-intentioned effort ended up promoting corruption in that district, while having little effect in improving security there:

"Nuristanis are getting money from [ISAF] for local projects and pocketing most of it, without working to fulfill the projects and improve the community. The recipients have the attitude that project funds are 'infidel money' and therefore can be used however they want, because contracts with 'infidels' are not valid. Furthermore, the district *shura* demands that [ISAF] not hire outside contractors, compelling [ISAF] personnel to give funds to the *shura* itself. The *shura* members then just split the money among themselves."

Efforts to improve communication between ISAF and local leaders should be encouraged, but with better verification of the reputation and productivity of people who present themselves as such leaders.

CROSS-BORDER INFILTRATION AND RELATIONS WITH PAKISTAN

Nuristan's eastern border with Pakistan's Chitral district continues to be an area of cross-border infiltration for jihadists wishing to join the insurgency. Insurgents maintain supply lines over key passes from Chitral to cells operating in the highland forests of Kamdesh district, and they freely cross through Bargi Matal district, despite the presence of ANP personnel there. Other supply routes through Kunar serve insurgents operating elsewhere in the province.

Relations between Nuristanis and Pakistanis from Chitral are generally good, as many Nuristanis spent the Soviet war years as refugees there. Nuristanis travel freely across the border to seek medical services or shop in Chitral.

The people of Nisheygram, Waygal District, prepare a feast. Men herd their animals throughout the year, taking them into the alpine pastures in the spring, back to the village in the fall, down to the lower valleys in the winter, and into the pastures in the summer.

PHOTO BY DAVID KATZ

Appendices

TIMELINE OF KEY EVENTS

October 1978: Afghanistan's first sustained grassroots revolt against its communist government begins in eastern Nuristan.

Early 1980's: The grassroots insurgency is co-opted by ISI-sponsored Islamist parties, with HIG predominant by the time the communist government falls in 1992.

Autumn 2002: ISAF troops make first forays into Nuristan; jihadists there go underground.

2003-2005: Jihadist insurgents launch numerous attacks on vehicular traffic and NGOs in Nuristan, causing delays and shutdowns of development projects. By 2005 most assistance organizations have left eastern Nuristan.

2006: ISAF troops set up a presence at numerous outposts in the province, along with ANA counterparts. An attempt to install a PRT facility in Kamdesh district is abandoned because of its indefensible location, and Nuristan's PRT remains at Kala Gush in the province's southwest.

2007: Attempts by ISAF personnel to secure closer ties with the people of eastern Nuristan begin to look promising, with the creation of a "100-man shura," but diminished follow-through leads to stagnation.

September 2007: A special-forces raid in Pitigal kills 5 insurgents and 14 civilians

April 2008: 17 civilians are killed in raid on Shuk in Doab district

June 2008: A truckload of fleeing civilians is killed by a coalition airstrike on the road Waygal district

July 2008: A firefight at Want in Waygal district kills 17 OEF soldiers; afterward elders from Waygal district ask ISAF to cease all operations in their district.

July 2008: Governor Tamim Nuristani is replaced by Hazrat Din Nur, who was killed in a road accident two months later.

November 2008: Jamaluddin Badr is appointed governor.

COMMON COMPLIMENTS REGARDING THE US MILITARY IN THE EASTERN REGION

- Afghans respect the US forces for leaving their families to come and help them.

- Afghans compliment the US forces' work ethic and say it drives them to work harder for themselves.

- Afghans are happy for projects such as roads that change their lives for the better after decades of war.

- Other foreign armies have come to conquer; the US military has come to help Afghans.

COMMON COMPLAINTS REGARDING THE US MILITARY IN THE EASTERN REGION

- Afghans claim that when US troops are attacked by insurgents, they sometimes retaliate against innocent people.

- Afghans claim that ISAF has inflicted excessive civilian casualties while taking out few insurgent leaders.

- Afghans complain that the US forces raid their houses at night without cause or government support.

- Afghans believe US troops use informers for their intelligence gathering who are not being honest. Most of these people have their own agendas and manipulate the truth.

- Afghans lament that ISAF troops and other foreign personnel do not know or understand the local people and what is going on among them.

- Afghans complain that US forces drive them off the roads and drive too carelessly.

DAY IN THE LIFE OF A NURISTANI

The schedule of daily life in Nuristan depends on the season. People rise before dawn to offer the first of their five daily prayers. Women build a fire over which they cook flat loaves of bread on a convex griddle. Breakfast typically consists of bread mashed in milk, or bread with cheese or curds, washed down with milk tea. During the spring and summer growing season, the women set out to the fields to spend their day weeding, fertilizing, and irrigating. Before noon they pause to eat a small snack of bread and say their midday prayers before returning to their arduous agricultural work. At dusk they return home to cook dinner, which usually consists of more bread with a dairy product. In the spring wild greens supplement the meal; later in the season beans, peas, and squash are also eaten.

Men are in charge of the livestock, which are herded in a yearly cycle that takes them from the village to the alpine pastures in the spring, back to the village in the fall, and to lower valley quarters in the winter. During the summer months they spend their days in the pastures, herding the goats on their daily grazing rounds and producing the various types of cheese and curds derived from the animals' milk. Several men will pool their livestock and manpower resources, taking turns with the chores.

During the fall women spend their days gathering firewood for the next season's heating and cooking. In winter months, after harvesting and settling in, daily life slows. Women tend to household chores; men hang out around the mosque or with friends, often playing games like quoits or field hockey.

FURTHER READING AND SOURCES

See the topics "The Current Political Situation in Nuristan," "Peoples and Languages of Nuristan," "The True Story of Our Jihad," and others on the web at: Richard Strand's Nuristan Site: *http://users.sedona. net/~strand*

Books

- *ISAF PRT Handbook*, 3rd Ed. NATO, February 2007.

- Louis Dupree, *Afghanistan*, Princeton: Princeton University Press, 1979. (Available in paperback. Offers an excellent understanding of the code of Pashtuns. Understand Pashtunwali and you will be successful.)

- Edward Girardet and Jonathan Walter, *Afghanistan: Essential Field Guides to Humanitarian and Conflict Zones,* CROSSLINES Publication Ltd., 1998 and 2004; www.crosslinesguides.com.

- Ahmed Rashid, *Descent into Chaos: The United States and the Future of Nation Building in Afghanistan, Pakistan, and Central Asia,* Viking Press, 2008.

- Ahmed Rashid, *Taliban: Militant Islam, Oil and Fundamentalism in Central Asia,* 2001.

- Larry Goodson, *Afghanistan's Endless War: State Failure, Regional Politics, and the Rise of the Taliban,* 2001.

- Greg Mortenson, *Three Cups of Tea: One Man's Mission to Promote Peace... One School at a Time,* 2007. (Excellent understanding of how to succeed with the people and culture.)

- Barnett Rubin, 1) *The Fragmentation of Afghanistan,* and 2) *Afghanistan's Uncertain Transition from Turmoil to Normalcy,* 2001 and 2007.

- Michael Griffin, *Reaping the Whirlwind: The Taliban Movement in Afghanistan,* London: Pluto Press, 2001.

- Steve Coll, G*host Wars: The Secret History of the CIA, Afghanistan, and Bin Laden, From the Soviet Invasion to September 10, 2001,* New York: Penguin Press, 2004.

- Marc Sageman, *Understanding Terrorist Networks,* Philadelphia: University of Pennsylvania Press, 2004.

Articles and Documents

- *Provincial Survey of Nuristan*, by Katarina Larsson, Swedish Committee of Afghanistan, May 2006.

- The Afghanistan National Development Strategy, President Karzai, 2006, *www.reliefweb.int/rw/RWFiles2006.nsf/FilesByRWDocUNIDFileName/ KHII-6LK3R2-unama-afg-30jan2.pdf/$File/unama-afg-30jan2.pdf*

- *Potential Analysis of the Eastern Region and Nangarhar Province and Implication in Programming*, Raphy Favre, *www.aizon.org/ Nangarhar%20Potential%20Analysis.pdf*

- *Mines and Mineral Occurrences of Afghanistan,* compiled by G.H. Orris and J.D. Bliss, open-file report 02-110, US Geological Survey, US Department of the Interior, 2002.

- *National Risk and Vulnerability Survey 2005*, Central Statistics Office. *http://cso-af.net/nrva2005/Docs_Reports.php*

- *Nuristan Natural Resource Assessment,* International Foundation of Hope, Report for USAID/ LGCD RFP No. RFP-JLB-NINF-001, 2009.

Web Sites

- Afghanistan Research and Evaluation Unit (publishes the Afghanistan A to Z guide), *www.areu.org.af/index.php?option=com_frontpage& Itemid=25* (You can download the well-known Afghan A-Z Guide on this site)

- Afghanistan Information Management Services, *www.aims.org.af*

- Afghanistan Online (Links to Official IRA and embassy websites), *www.afghan-web.com/politics*

- Naval Postgraduate School Program for Culture and Conflict Studies, *www.nps.edu/Programs/CCS/index.html*

- USAID, *www.usaid.gov/locations/asia/countries/afghanistan*

- Richard Strand's Nuristan Site, *http://users.sedona.net/~strand*